Daring Women
of the American Revolution

Francis Walsh

The Rosen Publishing Group's
PowerKids Press™
New York

Published in 2009 by The Rosen Publishing Group, Inc.
29 East 21st Street, New York, NY 10010

Copyright © 2009 by The Rosen Publishing Group, Inc.

Book Design: Haley W. Harasymiw

Photo Credits: Cover, pp. 5, 11, 12, 22, 25 © Hulton Archive/Getty Images; pp. 3, 4, 6, 9, 10, 13–15, 17, 18–20, 23–24, 26, 28–32 (flag background) © Gordan/Shutterstock; pp. 7, 9 (stamp) courtesy of Carmel Historical Society; p. 15 http://en.wikipedia.org/wiki/Image:Abigail_Adams.jpg; p. 16 © Time & Life Pictures/Getty Images; p. 19 http://en.wikipedia.org/wiki/Image:Mercy_Otis_Warren.jpg; p. 21 http://en.wikipedia.org/wiki/Image:MollyPitcher.jpeg; p. 27 © The Palma Collection/Photodisc/Getty Images; p. 29 courtesy of North Carolina Archives.

Library of Congress Cataloging-in-Publication Data

Walsh, Francis, 1953-
  Daring women of the American Revolution / Francis Walsh.
      p. cm. - (Real life readers)
  Includes index.
  ISBN: 978-1-4358-0177-6 (paperback)
  6-pack ISBN: 978-1-4358-0178-3
  ISBN 978-1-4358-2994-7 (library binding)
 1. United States—History—Revolution, 1775-1783—Women—Juvenile literature. 2. United States—History—Revolution, 1775-1783—Biography—Juvenile literature. 3. United States—History—Revolution, 1775-1783—Participation, Female—Juvenile literature. 4. Women—United States—History—18th century—Juvenile literature. 5. Women—United States—Biography—Juvenile literature. I. Title.
  E276.W34 2009
  973.3082-dc22
                              2008039565

Manufactured in the United States of America

Contents

A Time for Bravery

In the 1700s, the British government made laws for the American colonists without giving them any control over how they were governed. Many colonists grew unhappy with British rule. They decided to fight for independence. The American Revolution was fought between 1775 and 1783. You've learned about many American heroes already, such as George Washington and Paul Revere. Have you ever heard of any female heroes of the American Revolution?

During the late 1700s, women took care of the home and children. They had to dress and behave in a certain way. They weren't supposed to take part in wars and politics. However, many daring women knew they could help fight, too. Some fought with guns, while others used their special abilities. All of these women helped bring about an American victory in the war.

This picture shows the Battle of Bunker Hill in 1775. Although the British won, the American colonists believed they could win their independence if they continued to fight.

Sybil Ludington

In 1777, Sybil Ludington was 16 years old. She lived with her family near Fredericksburg, New York. Her father, Colonel Henry Ludington, was the leader of a local **militia**. Sybil was the oldest of twelve children, and she worked hard to help take care of her brothers and sisters.

On April 26, 1777, a messenger arrived at the Ludingtons' house in the middle of the night. He told Sybil's father that British troops were attacking nearby Danbury, Connecticut, where many military supplies were kept. Someone needed to gather the militia to fight the British and save their supplies. The messenger was tired from his journey and didn't know the area. Sybil knew where her father's men could be found. Although it was dangerous, she asked her father to let her spread the news. He agreed.

This statue of Sybil Ludington
is found in Carmel, New York.

Sybil's Ride: Cause and Effects

EFFECT: George Washington thanked Sybil for her brave action.

EFFECT: Militia forced British forces back to their ships.

EFFECT: Sybil's town honored her by renaming the town Ludingtonville.

CAUSE: Sybil Ludington rode all night to gather her father's militia together.

EFFECT: Each year, people follow Sybil's route to remember her courage.

EFFECT: Sybil was honored with a stamp and a statue.

Sybil rode her horse all night. She traveled about 40 miles (64 km) through hard rain. Luckily, she didn't meet any British troops.

"Muster at Ludington's!" shouted Sybil at the houses of the militia members. This meant that the soldiers were to meet at her father's house. Over 400 men had gathered by the time Sybil, wet and tired, completed her ride at dawn. The militia was too late to save Danbury, but they forced the British back toward their ships.

Sybil's story spread. George Washington even thanked her! Some people called her the "Girl Paul Revere." Sybil Ludington's town was later named Ludingtonville to honor her bravery. Each year in April, people walk or run along the path that Sybil took and remember the historic ride of a young woman.

This Sybil Ludington stamp made in 1975 honors her role in the American Revolution.

Deborah Samson

Deborah Samson was born around 1760 to a poor family in Massachusetts. She became an **indentured servant** at a young age. Deborah worked for the Thomas family and learned many skills in both the farm fields and the house. She never went to school, but the Thomas children taught her reading, writing, and other things they learned at school. Deborah learned quickly. She learned so well that she became a teacher after she finished her years of work for the Thomases.

By that time, Deborah heard about the battles being fought in the American Revolution. She wanted to help the colonies, but their army, called the Continental army, didn't allow women to be soldiers. What could Deborah do?

Deborah finished working for the Thomas family in 1778 but stayed with them for a few more years.

11

In 1782, Deborah **disguised** herself as a man and joined the Continental army. She called herself Robert Shurtliff. When Deborah was hurt in battle, she didn't let doctors tend all her wounds. She was afraid they would discover she was a woman and make her leave the army. Deborah suffered from her untreated wounds for the rest of her life. In 1783, a military doctor discovered Deborah was a woman after she fell sick with a fever. This was the end of her army career.

Deborah married and raised a family. She told her adventures to others. With Paul Revere's help, she also fought to receive payment for her time as a soldier. After many years, she was finally given pay and recognized as a true Continental soldier.

This picture shows Deborah Samson delivering a message to George Washington (seated). Some people say that Deborah met Washington and that he kept her secret.

Abigail Adams

Not all the daring women of the American Revolution used their hands to fight. Some used words and pens! Abigail Adams was one of these women. Abigail, born in 1744 in Massachusetts, loved to read and taught herself about many subjects. She became the wife of John Adams, a founding father of the United States who became the country's second president.

Abigail wrote many letters to John when he went to Philadelphia, Pennsylvania, to meet with the other members of the **Continental Congress**. He often asked her opinion about matters of government and politics. During the war, Abigail's letters included facts about where British troops and ships were placed in Boston. These letters helped John and the colonial forces plan how to fight their enemies.

This picture of Abigail was painted in 1766, 2 years after she married John Adams.

he has distinguished himself in every engagement, by his cou[rage]
and fortitude, by animating the soldiers & leading them on by his o[wn]
example — a particular account of these dreadful, but I hope glo[rious]
Days will be transmitted you, no doubt in the exadest manner —

The race is not to the Swift, nor the
battle to the Strong — but the God of Israll is he that giveth Strength & pow[er]
unto his people. Trust in him at all times ye people pour out your hearts
before him, God is a refuge for us — Charlstown is laid in ashes. The Battle
began upon our intrenchments upon Bunkers Hill, a Saturday morning
about 3 oclock & has not ceased yet & tis now 3 oclock Sabbath afternoon

Tis expected they will come out over the
Neck to night & a dreadful battle must ensue almighty God cover
the heads of our Country men — & be a shield to our dear Friends how
many have fallen we know not, the constant roar of the cannon is
so distressing that we cannot eat Drink or Sleep — may we be supported
and sustained in the dreadful conflict — I shall tarry here till tis thought
unsafe by my Friends & then I have secured myself a retreat at your
Brothers who has kindly offerd me part of his House — I cannot compose
myself to write any further at present — I will add more as I hear
further —

Tuesday afternoon —

I have been so much agitated that I have not been able to write
since Sabbeth Day — when I say that ten thousand reports are passing
vague & uncertain as the wind I believe I speak the truth — I am
not able to give you ...

John Adams was called to the Second Continental Congress in 1776. He and several other leaders were given the task of writing the Declaration of Independence. This important paper stated that the colonies were free from British rule. Abigail sent John a letter asking him to "remember the ladies" as laws were being created for the new country. She didn't believe it was fair to give all the power to men. Women deserved rights as well.

Abigail also believed that slavery was wrong. She argued that the United States could never be a country that stood for freedom until all people were truly free. Although women and blacks wouldn't be given equal rights until much later, Abigail is considered a hero for voicing her beliefs in equality for all.

Mercy Otis Warren

In 1728, Mercy Otis Warren was born into a colonial family that was strongly against British rule. Although Mercy didn't go to school, she learned to read and write at home. She married James Warren in 1754, and they both became very active in the American Revolution.

Known for her intelligence, Mercy **corresponded** with famous leaders, such as Samuel Adams, John Hancock, Thomas Jefferson, and George Washington. She was a good friend to both Abigail and John Adams, who encouraged her to write her views.

Abigail Adams
- sent letters about where British forces were gathered
- argued against slavery

BOTH
- wrote letters to famous American leaders
- argued for women's rights

Mercy Otis Warren
- wrote against British colonial rule
- first American woman to write plays

Mercy decided to write plays to convince others to fight British rule. Although the plays weren't performed, many people read them. Those plays made Mercy the first American female **playwright**. Mercy also wrote poetry and books about the events of the Revolution.

Like Abigail Adams, Mercy Otis Warren worked for women's rights.

Molly Pitcher

Molly Pitcher is one of the best-known female heroes of the American Revolution. However, Molly Pitcher was not a real name! In fact, Molly Pitcher may represent several women's stories combined into one person.

Many of Molly Pitcher's stories might be based on Mary Ludwig. Mary was born near Philadelphia, Pennsylvania, around 1754. She married William Hays, a barber who signed up for the Continental army during the American Revolution. At that time, women often traveled with their husbands and cooked, washed, and sewed for the American soldiers. For their work, they received half the amount of **rations** that soldiers received. Mary, like other poor women, decided to travel with her husband.

Was Mary Ludwig really Molly Pitcher?
This picture shows Molly preparing a cannon in battle.

The Battle of Monmouth was fought in New Jersey on June 28, 1778. The day was very hot. Mary carried **pitchers** of water into battle. Water was needed for the thirsty soldiers and, more importantly, to clean the cannons after each shot was fired. Some believe Mary got her famous name when people called out for more water. "Molly" is a nickname for "Mary," so the soldiers may have yelled, "Molly, pitcher!"

William fell ill from the heat during the battle. Mary took his place, helping fire the cannons. The Americans continued to fight until the British retreated. Beginning in 1822, Pennsylvania gave Mary $40 a year for her service. The bravery of "Molly Pitcher" became one of the most famous stories of the American Revolution.

Some say that George Washington made Mary an officer. She may have been called "Sergeant Molly"!

Betsy Ross

Betsy Ross was born in 1752. She and her husband, John, owned an **upholstery** shop in Philadelphia. John joined the Philadelphia militia but died in an explosion in 1776. Betsy was left to run the shop by herself and became known for her sewing skills. She may have sewed clothes for George Washington. She also became a flag maker for the Pennsylvania navy.

One story tells that George Ross visited Betsy in July 1776. He was her husband's uncle and had signed the Declaration of Independence. According to the story, George Washington came with him. They gave Betsy a drawing of a flag they wanted her to make. Some say Washington wanted stars with six points, but Betsy convinced him they should have five points. Betsy, as the story tells, soon completed the first American flag with stars and stripes. Congress made it the official flag of the United States in June 1777.

In this picture, Betsy Ross shows George Washington (left) and others the flag she created.

Polly Cooper

One of the colonial army's worst times of the American Revolution was the winter of 1777 through 1778 in Valley Forge, Pennsylvania. George Washington's army of about 10,000 men, discouraged after several losses, waited out the winter in log huts. The army didn't have enough money to clothe the men warmly or provide enough food. Over 2,000 soldiers died from the hard conditions.

More might have died if not for the actions of a Native American woman. Polly Cooper was one of several people sent by the Oneida chief with corn for the hungry army. Polly stayed and cooked for the soldiers. She taught them to make soup and medicine from the area plants. Polly refused to be paid for her work. She was given a special **shawl** that the Oneida people still have and which remains a sign of the friendship between the Oneida and the United States.

This painting shows an artist's idea of the mood and conditions of Washington's army in Valley Forge.

Penelope Barker

You've probably heard of the **Boston Tea Party**, but have you heard of the Edenton Tea Party? Edenton, North Carolina, was the home of Penelope Barker. Penelope's husband, Thomas, was in Britain during much of the American Revolution. Penelope remained at home to care for her family. Many believe that Penelope was responsible for organizing the women of her town in an important protest in 1774.

On October 25, fifty-one women signed a paper promising to **boycott** tea and cloth that was taxed by the British government. The boycott was a way to let the British leaders know of their unhappiness. The paper was even printed in London newspapers, shocking many British people. Many consider this the first political action organized by American women. They may not have been able to fight in other ways, but they used what power they had.

think Penelope Barker and the other Edenton women
re braver than the men of the Boston Tea Party. The
didn't disguise themselves and signed their real names.

Daring Women Make History

Women didn't stop taking part in important events after the American Revolution. More and more women began to go to school and prove that they could succeed in all areas of life. Women became doctors, lawyers, and soldiers. They finally got the right to vote in 1920. Today we can look back on history and see that many women didn't just watch historical events—daring women made history happen.

said to have made the first U.S. flag

gathered militia to fight British

disguised herself as a man to fight in Continental army

Betsy Ross

Sybil Ludington

Deborah Samson

helped soldiers and fought in battle

Molly Pitcher

Heroes of the American Revolution

Penelope Barker

organized women to boycott British goods

Abigail Adams

Mercy Otis Warren

Polly Cooper

provided facts about British forces

wrote plays against British colonial rule

helped Continental army at Valley Forge

Glossary

Boston Tea Party (BOS-tuhn TEE PAHR-tee) A protest against British taxes in 1773 in which disguised men threw tea into Boston Harbor.

boycott (BOY-kaht) To join with others in refusing to deal with a person, nation, or business to let them know that you don't approve of their actions.

Continental Congress (kahn-tuh-NEHN-tuhl KAHN-gruhs) One of three meetings of the leaders of the American colonies held before, during, and after the American Revolution.

correspond (kohr-uh-SPAHND) To exchange messages.

disguise (dihs-GYZ) To wear a costume or an outfit to hide who you are.

indentured servant (ihn-DEHN-shurd SUHR-vuhnt) A person who signs an agreement to work for another person for a set amount of time. In return, they receive payment of travel or living costs.

militia (muh-LIH-shuh) A group of citizens who are trained and ready to fight when needed.

pitcher (PIH-chuhr) Jug.

playwright (PLAY-ryt) Someone who writes plays.

ration (RAA-shun) An amount of something, such as food, given to people, especially during a time of war.

shawl (SHAWL) A piece of clothing worn by women over the shoulders or head.

upholstery (up-HOHL-stuh-ree) Cloth and sewing

Index

Due to the changing nature of Internet links, The Rosen Publishing Group, Inc., has developed an online list of Web sites related to the subject of this book. This site is updated regularly. Please use this link to access the list: http://www.rcbmlinks.com/rlr/daring